M000169113

FUCK YOU FUEL

How To Turn Shit Into Sugar

By

Barbie The Welder

You are Fucking powerful!

Love,

Barbie The Welder

Also written by Barbie The Welder

- Horseshoe Crafts; More Than 30 Easy Projects You Can Weld At Home
- The Inspiration Blueprint; How To Design & Create Your Inspired Life
- How To Weld Silverware Animals; Metal Art Welding Projects
- How To Weld Scrap Metal Art; 30 Easy Welding Projects You Can Make At Home
- Honor Thy Art; How To Be An Extremely
  - Successful Artist

Copyright © 2021 Barbie The Welder All rights reserved.
ISBN: 978-1-63795-993-0

DEDICATION

Dedicated with love to everyone who told me no, you can't do that, & it will never happen! Thank you for making me stronger!

ACKNOWLEDGMENTS

To my clients, supporters, fans, & followers

In the beginning Fuck You Fuel kept me powering through the hard times, but today I get that fuel from you! Your love and support fills my soul with joy and helps me push myself harder so together we can rise!

Thank you from the bottom of my heart! (That's the part with all the good love in it!)

With love and appreciation,

Barbie The Welder

🚀10

---◆◆◆---

You're scared. It's OK, it happens to all heroes. This is the part where you face the villain and win!

-Barbie The Welder

---◆◆◆---

I am fucking proud of you! I know the journey you're about to go on, a hero's journey, and I know the courage that it takes, and here you are you ballsy SOB, and **I love you** for it!

Fuck You Fuel is NOT about "not giving a fuck." It's actually the opposite! Fuck You Fuel is about giving so much of a fuck about yourself that you choose to take every negative in your life, flip it on its head, and use it for energy to accomplish your every dream, goal, and desire.

Fuck You Fuel is a mental strategy, a game you will learn to play. When you learn and implement this strategy you will change and shape your future, bend life to your very will! Say it with me! **This is Fucking Powerful!**

You are taught what to think in school but not HOW TO THINK. Everyone thinks, but if you're like most people, the majority of your thinking is chaotic, and you're constantly bombarded with thoughts. Most people lack the strategic aspect of thinking that allows us to grow and strengthen ourselves. What our thinking usually consists of is lying awake at night wanting to go to sleep but our brains are going over every scenario of the day, bouncing from one subject to another without direction. Runaway thoughts in an undisciplined mind is the truth of many people's existence. Left undisciplined, our thinking can cause stress, anxiety, depression, and low self-esteem, a personal shit storm.

Every human has two sides. One side is a leader, your alpha energy, a badass take charge motherfucker. The other side is a follower, your beta energy, someone who gets walked on. Don't think you have an alpha side? Let someone disrespect something or someone you love and see how that makes you feel! Even if you don't say anything out loud you still feel anger inside, that's your alpha energy, your power!

If your thoughts run nonstop that means up until now you've been a beta thinker, your brain is walking all over you. That's awesome because you will see the most incredible growth from Fuck You Fuel! For all you out there who control your thoughts, the alpha thinkers, you're going to love the results you get as you learn how to leverage Fuck You Fuel and be more strategic in your thinking!

You are a rocket, a fucking powerful missile! When a rocket is built soundly, pointed in the right direction, has a solid launch pad and the correct fuel to burn, the universe belongs to you! You can blast off to everything you've ever wanted to achieve, personally and financially!

Living a life that makes you happy heart and soul is your birthright, but it's up to you to go out and make it happen!

9

You only need one person to believe in

you and that's you! When you've

believed in yourself long enough you

will produce results and then people

will have no choice but to believe in

you!

Barbie The Welder

LIFE WILL REFLECT BACK TO YOU THAT WHICH YOU BELIEVE

Before you can BLAST OFF you need to make sure you, the rocket, is in perfect flying condition and your launch pad is solid. A rocket can be aimed in the right direction and have all the fuel in the world but if the rocket was duck taped together and the launch pad is fucked, it won't go half as far or in the right direction, and chances are it will blow the fuck up!

If you are the rocket, that makes your brain your launch pad. More than 6,000 thoughts are launched from our brains every day, and if we have not been doing maintenance on our launch pad our thoughts are going to be right fucked at times.

We need to get you and your launch pad ready for flight, and the way to do that is by looking at your **foundation of thought**, your current mental strategy, or lack of one! No judgments here, I spent most of my life with zero mental strategy, I believed everything people told me and had a fuck ton of excuses why I wasn't where I wanted to be, and you're damn right, it was everyone's fault except mine! It doesn't matter what you've done in the past, how you've handled or ignored things, it only matters that you realize that you can choose to make your life beyond incredible from here on out.

FUCK YOU FUEL

IT'S TIME TO QUESTION EVERYTHING!

We get input from everyone and everything in our life. From our parents, relatives, teachers, the government, commercials, the news, social media, the list goes on and on. The problem with the input we receive is that most of what comes in is never filtered or questioned and we simply file it away in our brains and then feed ourselves this input in the form of thoughts. When it's time for us to make a decision, that decision is based on all the input we've received, and not just current input, but input from the beginning of our lives to now.

Pretend for a moment you are a 5-year-old kid and you're joyfully singing a song at the top of your lungs! Your parent walks into the room and, unbeknownst to you they have a migraine headache.

Your parent is normally very loving but right now they're in pain and not thinking straight, and they tell you to shut up, that your voice is giving them a headache. As a little kid you don't understand what a migraine headache is and you have no idea they are in pain, so their hurtful words goes right to your heart and breaks it.

What happens to your 5 year old joyful self? You believe that your voice is so awful that it gives people headaches, and you decide to never sing again. Hell, you might even choose to talk quietly from now on so your voice won't hurt someone! Was your input accurate? ABSOLUTLY NOT! You didn't know the whole story! In your lack of ALL THE INFORMATION you spend the rest of your life BELIEVING you have an awful singing vice.

Another example: Your parent is late for an appointment and walking quickly across a parking lot dragging you along with them. In their rush they tell you to stop being so slow. Their legs are twice as long as yours, but your 5 year old self can't math yet so you take in the input that "you're slow". Do you think you would ever try out for the track team? Even if you love running and are faster than everyone on the playground you may spend the rest of your life believing you're slow, and not just in running, you may take it a step further and think you're slow, like as in learning disabled slow. It becomes part of who you are, "I'm slow."

This phenomenon doesn't just happen to us as kids, it happens all our lives! We wear a hat we love to a friend's house and the friend tells us we look awful in that hat. We believe we look awful in hats and never wear one again. We jump to conclusions never questioning the input. What if the friend had an alcoholic parent who wore a hat when they were abusive to them? How the hat looked on you had nothing to do with you, it was about the hat bringing back bad memories for that friend.

This happens again and again in our lives, we think we know all the information, we allow input into our brains and misjudge situation after situation. Some situations may work to our advantage, while others get misinterpreted. We then walk around with misinformation about us and the world around us, making decisions based on false information.

Because we never question the input our foundation of thought is all fucked up and we don't even know it!

How many beliefs have we held about ourselves that are simply untrue?

It's time to start questioning the input, and not just current input, we need to go all the way back as far as we can remember!

BLASTING OFF FROM A SOLID LAUNCH PAD

Find a way to take notes that will be private. Get yourself a notebook, take notes in your phone, get a journal, or do whatever works for you. Don't skip this shit! For fuck's sake, **you deserve massive success,** and the easiest way to create massive success is to work on the right shit. This is the right shit!

When you're working with this book shut off your phone's notifications and get yourself a quiet place to work, even if it's the shitter! If you work with constant distractions your thoughts will be scattered and you won't get the results you deserve. Decide to be in 100% or get the fuck out. Full sends only people! That should go for EVERY area of your life!

Our foundation needs to be solidly built on positive beliefs. So far we've been accepting whatever input comes our way without filtering it, but no more! It's time we root out the bullshit, the misinformation we've been accepting as truth!

In your notebook make a list of all the negative beliefs you hold about yourself. Examples:

I'm slow

A guy/girl can't _____

I don't deserve_____

I can never _____

I've got back luck

Single parents are poor

Artists are broke

I'm too old/young to _____

I'm not worthy of love because_____

I'm not smart

This always happens to me

I'm not capable

I'm a failure

No one's done it before so it's impossible

You can't teach an old dog new tricks

I'm bad with money

I'm a chicken

I'm not worthy

I'm not valuable

I'm a klutz

I can never find someone who will love me

Really take your time and think on this. You may find that as you go through your week more things will come to you and when they do write them down! We've held some of these beliefs for so long we don't even realize we have them, we just run on autopilot making decisions based on what we think is true!

Now, I don't give a fuck where these beliefs come from, but I do give a fuck about getting rid of them, and trust me, we are going to get rid of them! They have not served you positively, and it's time they stop renting space in your head.

Our brain is a belief engine. Once a belief is formed it goes to work finding proof that supports your belief, it needs to "be right." When it finds proof, that proof reinforces the belief making the belief stronger. Round and round it goes creating a self-fulfilling prophecy, a nasty ass merry go round that shits on you ever time you complete the circle. If my belief is "I'm not smart" my brain goes to work coming up with every fucked up thing I've done to reinforce that belief! The longer we've held a belief the easier it is for our brain to find proof, and the stronger that belief becomes.

We don't need to lay down on a sofa and do the therapist thing to get rid of our negative beliefs, we just need to play a game I call Mumbo Jumbo.

Pick a negative belief you wrote down. I'm going to use "I'm not smart" as my example to walk you through what to do next.

Write the negative belief at the top of a new page. As you write you will notice that your brain will immediately begin listing all the "reasons" that support that negative belief, that's Mumbo Jumbo, and it's our job to ignore it!

We are going to take that old belief and fuck it up. We know our brain needs to be right, so in order to turn this negative belief on its head and make it positive we need to create new references. This is your hero's journey!

Draw a thick line through your negative belief and write the opposite underneath it. It should look like this:

~~I'm not smart~~

I'm smart

Brainstorm and write down all the times in your life you made a smart move. Did you leave an ex who was abusive?

Even if it took you 10 years to leave, you suffered unmentionable abuse at their hands and you feel "not smart" for staying all that time, it was a smart move to leave and I need you to only focus on the smart move.

Continue brainstorming until you have at least 5 times in your life you can reference where you made smart moves and write them down under your new positive belief. It should look like this.

~~I'm not smart~~

I'm smart

- I left my abusive ex
- I saved my bonus check instead of pissing it away
- I left the bar after two drinks instead of drinking all night
- Instead of yelling at my kid when I was angry I took the time to walk away and think about what I should say.
- I fixed my car when it first started having a problem instead of letting it go until it became a major problem.

The game you will play from now on is to "catch" yourself every time your old negative belief creeps up and replace it with the new positive belief. When I say catch yourself I mean without judgment, no shitting on yourself for the old negative belief. Simply redirect your thought to any or all of your new positive beliefs! This is a game, so find a fun way to catch yourself that makes you laugh, it's more powerful and positive!

Example:

Thought: I just failed that test, I'm dumb.

Catch Yourself: Oh hell no Mumbo Jumbo, get that shit outta here! ReFuckingJected!

Redirected Thought: I'm smart because I left my ex. I failed the test because I didn't spend enough time studying. Next time I will study until I understand the information and easily pass the test.

Notice I used my new positive thought but didn't ignore the fact I failed the test. When we make mistakes we need to take full responsibility for them. It wasn't the teachers' fault, my loud roommate, or any number of excuses I could have used; I am personally responsible for everything in my life. If my roommate is loud I can ask them to quiet their shit down or find another place to study. If I chose to study around a noisy roommate and fail the test that's my fault, not the roommates.

Taking responsibility for EVERYTHING in your life puts the POWER in your hands to change everything! When we blame others we give that power away. Fuck that!

Own your shit without beating yourself up for it and come up with a way to never let that shit happen again.

Go back to your list of negative beliefs and write down each belief, cross it out, and come up with at least 5 examples that support your new positive belief. Have patience with yourself as you learn to play this new game. You will find that it becomes easier the more you play.

Keep your notes with you at all times at first so you can continue to reference them until your positive thoughts become your new beliefs and they automatically pop into your head when you are thinking about something.

Playing Mumbo Jumbo is the single most powerful thing you can do for yourself! When we question our beliefs and change the negative into positive it changes our entire foundation of thought, raises our self-esteem, and creates a new picture of ourselves! We attract into our life what we feel we deserve. When you think positive about yourself you attract positive things, surround yourself with positive people, and make decisions that will enhance your life. It's simple but fucking lifechanging!

At the end of each chapter you will find a new belief to add to your list of positive beliefs. Write your new belief down and come up with at least 5 examples to support this new positive belief.

8

---◆—◆—◆---

Shit happens to everyone, the only difference between genuinely happy people and everyone else is how they choose to respond when shit happens!

-Barbie The Welder

---◆—◆—◆---

If you study the stories of the greats, the people who are the **happiest and most successful**, you will find a common thread runs between them, all of them had to overcome a massive personal hell to get where they are. The people I've met who've gone through some of the most insane shit you can imagine are the most beautiful human beings, generous, kind, loving, and compassionate people. I believe there's something about walking through fire that creates a spectacular love and strength in a person, they know how it feels to live in hell and feel deeply grateful to not be there, but also feel a personal responsibility to help others who currently are. They are the people you see out there raising others up, helping, and giving back.

Shit happens and every single one of us have moments of hell in our lives, situations we experience that affect us negatively, cause hurt, anger, hate, frustration, and resentment. It could be someone not believing in you, the death of a loved one, a cancer diagnosis, addiction, a hater, or any number of negative things life throws at us.

Everyone experiences hell in one of two ways.
The first way: A person walks into hell, looks around, rents an apartment, stays for a while, maybe a week, maybe a few months, and then they move on.

The second way: A person walks into hell, looks around, buys a home, puts up a white picket fence, strings up Christmas lights on the front porch, sings "Tis the season to be angry," at the top of their lungs, and makes it their permanent residence.

We all have a story; shit we've been through that's made us who we are. Some have overcome insanely challenging situations while others have overcome less challenging situations, but, what one person feels is horrifying another person may look at it and say I wish my life was that easy.

No matter how freaking incredible a person's life looks, they too, have walked through or lived in hell during their lives, or are currently living in hell and just using really great filters on Instagram.

Just like me, I know you have a fuck ton of events and situations that have happened in your life that are shitty. GOOD! I know you're sitting there right now thinking Barbie is 2 beers short of a 12 pack but let me explain!

The fuel we will use to power our rocket is the energy we are going to reap from everything negative that happened to us in our past, our Fuck You Fuel! We are going to take every one of those shitty situations and turn each and every one of them into fuel to power that badass rocket that you are! The more shitty experiences you've had, the more fuel you will receive, more fuel = BIGGER BLASTOFF, and bigger blastoff = more success!

Ever have anyone tell you the worse your past is the more success you can have in the future? Well here I am telling you that shit is TRUTH, I've lived it and met many others who live it, and now it's your turn to live it!

LET'S GET DOWN AND DIRTY!

Get your notebook back out, start a new page, and at the top of the page write your name followed by Fuck You Fuel.

This is going to be slightly uncomfortable at first, like a prostate exam, but as you see the power this is going to give you it will become more like a treasure hunt, you know, a prostate exam with a happy ending!

FUCK YOU FUEL

Write down every negative thing that's ever happened to you, **every fucking thing**. You're not in this alone, I'm right here with you and I'll go first. The list that follows is true, I've been through some fucked up shit, but it's the absolute secret to my success, and I'm going to show you how all your fucked up shit will be the secret to your success too!

Barbie's Fuck You Fuel

- Bullied from the time I was 5 until I was 16
- Used drugs and alcohol by 15
- Pregnant at 16 and raised my son with no financial or emotional support from his father.
- Suicidal thoughts and depression was my everyday life by 17. I hated myself.
- Alcoholic and drug addict by the time I was 19
- 1st divorce by 21
- Homeless at 21 and left my son with my parents because I had no way to support him
- Checked myself in to the Behavior Science Unit to get off drugs

- Anger led to violence when I sobered up which got me locked up in the Psych Center, and my doctor told me I would never get out. (Wrong answer motherfucker!)

- Spent 2-3 fuzzy years doped up on Dr. prescribed medication because of my past addiction/depression

- Was doubted by my entire family when I told them I was going to be a sculptor

- 2nd divorce

- Ex refused to pay child support, now I'm raising two boys without financial support

- Was told by an asshat at the Small Business Bureau that I would never succeed as an artist when I went for business advice

- Beat up by a boyfriend when he was done using me for money

Your list may not be as harsh as mine or it may be way worse, there's no judgment here, everyone's shit is shitty. What matters is that you make a complete list of everything you can think of that was negative in your past, or present. Every time someone told you no, you were left out of all the reindeer games, denied for a raise, left at the altar, whatever it is put it on the list.

Now that you have your list I want you to deeply understand this; this list is not who you are or even who you were, these are things that happened to you, and YOU get to define how they shape you.

THE POOR ME GAME

The Poor Me Game is when something happens to you and you complain for days, weeks, or even years about how someone done did you wrong.

It's the reason you're broke, unhappy, unloved, can't get a good job, can't live where you want, blah blah blah...you fill in the blank!

How do I know about the Poor Me Game? I played it for years, and I was damn good at it if you ask me! I blamed everyone but myself for the shitty shape that my life was in.

When you play the Poor Me Game you give all your power away, you put the blame everywhere else instead of taking personal responsibility for your situation. When you blame others you can't change anything because we all know we can't change others, but when you take personal responsibility for something you are in control therefore you can make changes.

I'm not saying that it's alright for someone to physically abuse you, what I am saying is I made the choice to enter into a relationship even though there were red flags, hell, the guy was a walking red flag! It's fucked up that it happened, and at the time I was fucking devastated and blamed my ex, but when I chose to stop playing the Poor Me Game and look at the facts, I realized the part I was responsible for. It was humbling at first, but it became empowering once I focused on how much Fuck You Fuel I received from this situation. I made the decision to never let it happen again, set high standards for a relationship and today I'm in a relationship that is beyond incredible with a man who treats me with the love and respect that I deserve!

What don't kill you will make you stronger if you're willing to look at the part you play and DECIDE to never let it happen again. Lessons people, lessons.

Even if you've been playing the Poor Me Game with any or all of the things on your list you can choose to redefine how you look at them right now, take responsibility for your actions, and decide to let each and every situation make you stronger and smarter.

All that shit is in your past. Can we change the past? Not unless you've invented a fucking time machine since I wrote this book. If we can't change the past the next best thing we can do is learn how to use all our negative shit and make it fuel for success.

If you are currently going through anything on your list please address that as soon as possible. Get the support you need from whomever you need to and get that shit into your past as soon as possible so you can move on to the greatness you deserve! If you don't have support email me at BarbieTheWelder@GMail.com and I will be the support you need. Don't email me and play The Poor Me game, I'm a problem solver not a drama queen. I'll ask you questions that will get you solving your own problems and empower you to be your own problem solver.

Now, just because we are taking personal responsibility for our part doesn't mean were happy about this shit! Taking personal responsibility is about owning our power and having control of our lives! When we own our power we have the ability to make the changes necessary to give us the fucking epic lives that we deserve!

NEW BELIEF

It feels fucking epic to be responsible for my life!

7

You are not a fairy princess in a Disney

Movie, no one's coming to rescue you,

it's up to you to rescue your damn

self.

Barbie The Welder

WE'RE ANGRY AND WE'RE NOT GOING TO TAKE IT ANYMORE!

People are going to rip me a new asshole for this but fuck em' if they can't take a joke!

Fuck You Fuel is about leveraging your anger. Anger is powerful energy and energy is neither good nor bad, it just is. The longer you've been angry about a situation the more energy, fuel, you have built up. More fuel = more power, more power = bigger blast off, bigger blast off = more success!

Yes, we've taken personal responsibility for the shitty shit that happened to us but that doesn't mean the anger fades away, it's still there. If left unchecked our anger grows stronger with every passing day and eventually will consume us affecting every area of our lives, so it needs to be released.

FUCK YOU I WIN!

It's time to leverage our anger and use that energy positively! Back to our Fuck You Fuel list. For every item on your list I want you to tell it: FUCK YOU I WIN!

If you've got a roommate or neighbors who live close by you might want to do this in your head or under your breath, but if you can, without freaking anyone out, say it loud, say it proud!!

FUCK YOU FUEL

When you say, "FUCK YOU I WIN" it's a message to the Universe that you are going to take this event, and every other obstacle put in your way, and turn it into fuel to rocket yourself to success.

FUCK YOU I WIN is about empowerment, not anger. Yes, we use our energy from our anger to say it, but we are saying it with the intention of empowering ourselves to overcome that situation, not to get angrier.

Smile when you say FUCK YOU I WIN, feel fucking great about saying FUCK YOU I WIN! Know that every time you say FUCK YOU I WIN to a situation you are gaining more and more power over it, more control over your life. When you take control over your life you get to decide how your life is going to look instead of just holding on for the ride and hoping for the best.

This exercise is so simple yet so fucking powerful! Choosing how we respond to a situation instead of blindly reacting to hurtful things people do or say is empowering!

Our circumstances don't make us who we are, our choices do! When we choose to win no matter the situation we take our power back, give ourselves a lifetime supply of fuel, and are fucking unstoppable!

NEW BELIEF

I win!

6

Behind every challenge will be another challenge. Don't be the person wishing for an easy life, grow yourself into a person who thrives on overcoming obstacles!

Barbie The Welder

Even though we've learned how to say FUCK YOU I WIN to our old situations doesn't mean new shitty situations won't keep happening. The beautiful thing about being in the practice of saying "FUCK YOU I WIN!" to our old situations is that when new shitty situations happen we will automatically tell it "FUCK YOU I WIN!" The more we practice the better we'll get!

When we're living in anger and resentment over past situations we are level 1 or 2 people, not filtering our beliefs or controlling our lives. As we learn to filter our thoughts, question our beliefs, and take control of our lives we grow in higher level people.

When you're a level 1 or 2 person and you face a level 2 or 3 problem it's going to seem like a huge problem! How do you think a level 2 or 3 problem looks to a level 5 person? It hardly registers! How do you think a level 7 problem looks to a level 9 or 10 person? As a level 10 person a problem that would have you curled up in the corner sucking your thumb and shitting your pants if you were a level 2 person is no big fucking deal to you!

By working on and practicing the exercises above you're well on your way to being a level 3-4 person! That's exciting news because all those lower level problems won't even register with you and that makes for a much easier, less stressful life! But wait, there's more!

As a level 1-5 person there's still anger. The higher the level person you grown yourself into the less anger you feel until one day you have grown into a level 10 and life is motherfucking exquisite beyond anything you can ever imagine! Zero anger, zero frustration, zero stress, life is literally a bowl of fucking cherries!

Like a rocket we need all our anger energy in the beginning to blast off. We've lived with our beliefs most of our lives and in order to get out of the habit of living in false beliefs, blaming, complaining, and singing poor me we need to harness as much Fuck You Fuel as possibly. We need practice.

This is not a one and done exercise. Run down your list several times a day saying, "FUCK YOU I WIN!" to each and every situation. Breaking old habits takes patience and practice to overcome. Continue this exercise until it becomes a habit to say, "FUCK YOU I WIN!" each and every time a negative thought or situation comes up.

The more often you do this exercise the sooner you will see powerful results in your life.

NEW BELIEF

I am growing myself into a level 10 person!

5

*Looking back, I realize that every time
I was told no, or my idea was
rejected, it provided me with the fuel
to keep going.*

Barbie The Welder

I didn't understand the power of Fuck You Fuel until I stopped needing to say, "Fuck You!" to anyone who had fucked me over or held me back. I used it on and off for a few years not realizing how it was empowering me to survive some very dark times in my life.

Early on in my career as a full time artist I had a couple experiences that, unbeknownst to me at the time, gave me the Fuck You Fuel I needed to become an incredibly

37

happy and very successful human being. At the time I was failing magnificently as an artist, so I went to the Small Business Bureau to ask for advice. The advice I got from the guy working there was to go back to my job, he told me that I would never make it as a full time artist.

What the fuck, you're supposed to give people guidance, not a death sentence! I was devastated and angry beyond belief. I though fuck this motherfucker I'll show him he's wrong! Soon after that a guy I was dating used me for the money I had saved up from my 9-5 job to support myself as a full time artist, and when my money was gone he choke slammed me into the windshield of his car. What a charmer!

I left. My self-esteem was built up enough to know he had lost the best thing that ever had or ever would happen to him, but my intense anger had me awake every night with some very premeditated thoughts. To say that I was a level 2 person at that time would be generous!

FUCK YOU FUEL

BUSTING THROUGH THE GRAVITATIONAL FIELD

Fuck You Fuel became a tool for me after that. I used it every day as I relentlessly worked 16-18 hour days in my garage 7 days a week for the next 3 years to prove to both those motherfuckers they were dead wrong. Fuck you very much I will thrive as an artist and fuck you very much you lost out on an incredible human being.

I was angry then but what a gift they both gave me! Had those situations not happened who knows how things would have turned out! You wouldn't be reading this book right now, that I know! What did eventually happen was because I was putting so much time into my business I started having small successes. Those successes started stacking up and I began having larger and larger success. As my business became more successful my self-esteem grew and my anger subsided, I was finding deep joy in creating and improving my skills. One day the anger wasn't there anymore. Today I feel nothing but gratitude to both those men for the fuel they provided to rocket myself and my business into a life that is out of this fucking world!

This is the journey that you will take. You will use your anger energy extensively in the beginning but over time you will gain momentum and find gratitude replacing anger.

It's a fucking beautiful experience when you feel it happening. It changes everything in your life, and not just you, but others around you will be positively affected as well!

Once we bust through the gravitational field gravity releases her pull on us and we begin to go further faster with less energy needed! Without realizing it, our "FUCK YOU I WIN" turns into "I WIN, thank you for making me stronger!" Gratitude for the energy we acquired from our situations becomes a daily norm, and so much more starts to happen within us!

NEW BELIEF

Thank you for making me stronger!

4

Be unapologetically who you are!
Not everyone is going to like you, but
then again not everyone has good
taste!

-Barbie The Welder

Our mission, now that we have broken through the gravitational field, is to work on growing ourselves into level 9 and 10 people, people who filter every thought, spend energy on empowering ourselves, and happily overcome any and all obstacles with patience and love!

We have gained tremendous momentum with our anger energy and things are starting to calm down. The anger isn't as angry, and we can see results showing up in our lives from our hard work. When we see positive results from our hard work it improves our confidence, we feel stronger, more powerful and in control, and this raises our self-esteem.

It's time to kick in the afterburners to give you a boost and keep you moving in the right direction. Afterburners = Self-esteem. Having great self-esteem is fucking mandatory for success. If you have low self-esteem you will never go after massive success because you simply won't believe you deserve it.

Back to our beliefs. We give ourselves exactly what we feel like we deserve. It shows in what we say, where we live, the relationships we're in, and the job we hold. Self-esteem and our beliefs go hand in hand when we improve one we improve the other. With the work we've been doing on our beliefs our self-esteem has been seeing improvements, but if we work on our self-esteem **and** our beliefs, we will be see better results faster!

FUCK YOU FUEL

FUCK YOU FUEL RULES FOR SELF ESTEEM

Own who the fuck you are!

I'm going to repeat my quote from the beginning of the chapter because it's worth repeating. Learn it, love it, own the fuck out of it, say it to yourself in front of the mirror every time you step in front of it. Say it loud, say it proud! *Be unapologetically who you are! Not everyone is going to like you, but then again not everyone has good taste!* How fucking boring would this world be if we all looked alike and loved the same stuff? Give me variety or give me death! You don't need anyone's permission to be you! You are a motherfucking masterpiece! The odds of you being on this earth are insane, yet here you are, a perfect miracle of creation!

Self-esteem, it's in the name!

NEVER look to anyone else for your SELF-esteem, it's yours and yours alone! Advertisers, friends, family, and random strangers online will all put their two cents in about how you SHOULD look, how your life SHOULD be, what car, house, or job you SHOULD have. Tell them to go SHOULD on themselves! Your opinion of you is the ONLY opinion that matters. If someone doesn't love the hat your wearing? Fuck em'! Your neighbor don't like your truck parked on your lawn? Fuck em'! You do you! (Fuck em' = ignore them, not flip them off!) You're not for everyone and that's OK!

Haters gonna hate!

If you have haters show up in your life it's a great sign! Haters show up because you have shined a light on their inadequacy, lack of trying, and failure to work to make their lives better. Their disrespect has nothing to do with you and everything to do with how they feel about themselves. Never take that personally! Shut haters up with success and a smile. No need for negativity here! In your head tell them thank you for making me stronger and use any anger you may feel towards them as more fuel for your rocket!

Just the facts!

Take time to look at the facts of your life without judgment. Do you love your home? Do you love your body? Do you love your relationships? Are your kids running the neighborhood like feral animals? Are you working for a boss you hate? If there's something you don't like, don't hate on it, just make plans to change it! (More about this later!)

Never judge your day 1 against someone's day 100!
Look to others to see where you want to be, but never judge yourself against them. Judge yourself against yourself and work each day to improve yourself against who you were the previous day.

Focus on your positive traits!
What we spend time and energy on expands. Choose to focus on the positive aspects of yourself and work to improve yourself in the areas that you want to improve.

If you suffer from low self-esteem like I did don't worry, it's a learnable skill! Just like anything else that's new, it will take practice! Have patience with yourself and work to improve. Baby steps, over time, will add up to giant leaps!

NEW BELIEF

I love who I'm growing into!

3

Success is the result of having a vision

so strong that obstacles, failure, and

loss only act as motivation!

Barbie The Welder

If you're anything like me you sucked at walking when you first tried! The first time you tried to crawl and fell flat on your face did someone tell you to give up? No! you were encouraged to try again! You failed again and again trying to crawl for the first time, and again when you went from crawling to walking. Yes, you fell, yes you got hurt, but you kept fucking going until one day you were running around terrorizing pets and pulling shit out of the cupboards!

Why were we smarter at 10 months old then we are as teenagers or adults? We didn't give a shit about what others thought of us back then. We knew we wanted the cookie on the table, so we did whatever it took to get there, and that meant bumps and bruises. Can we learn something from our 10-month-old selves? You're damn right we can!

FAIL FORWARD

How do you look at failure? Do you see it as the end? Do you feel that someone who tries and fails is a fucking loser, a disappointment? If you view failure as negative, chances are you will never try something new.

Let me redefine failure for you! What if I told you failure is feedback, failure is positive, and failure is not the end but merely a sign to look inside yourself and reflect on what must be done next in order to succeed. Failure is life giving you the direction you need to be successful; you just need to be openminded enough to get the message! Leverage your failure and learn from it!

When something doesn't work the way you expected it to it doesn't mean it can't be done, it just means it can't be done the way you tried and there's another way you need to try. You could be working with the wrong partner, not be working with the correct information, need to put more time into your project, or grow yourself into a stronger person mentally.

How do you know what will work? You might not know right away, but what's important is that you don't give up trying and you learn from ever attempt. You might try 10 different ways and all of them fail but you need to continue trying and failing forward. Each time something doesn't work look at the facts and see what parts worked and what needs improvement. When you start again use what worked, drop what didn't, and add something new.

The people who don't give up when they fail are the ones who will eventually win against all odds! Move from failure to failure improving yourself each time until you have a small success, and then another success. Eventually the small successes will add up to larger successes!

Believe in yourself and back your belief up with **action**!

NEW BELIEF

I win or I learn!

ꬍ2

I've learned how to become a

problem solver. It's allowed me to

create sculptures, build my business,

and grow myself into someone I love!

Barbie The Welder

MOTHERFUCKIN CHALLENGE ACCEPTED!

Chances are, if there's something you want to do but don't know how to do it, someone already has it figured out and they posted a video of how to do it on YouTube! You can find instructions on everything you've ever wanted to figure out from sex, to how to grow your social media channel, and if you look hard enough you can probably find how to grow your social media channel with sex! Information is so readily available today that solving problems is becoming easier and easier! You just have to go out and find it!

The difference between someone who is rich and someone who is poor or someone who is happy and someone who is sad is their problem-solving skills! Problem solving is an easy skill to learn. When you improve your problem solving skills, you improve your quality of life!

Problem solving is all about the questions you're asking yourself! Want better results in your life? Ask yourself better questions!

If you're asking yourself "Why does this always happen to me?" you are playing Poor Me and complaining, not problem solving! Asking yourself "How can I keep this from happening again?" is problem solving!

Any time you're faced with a situation you're not happy about get in the habit of asking yourself questions that will put you in problem solving mode!

Here is a list of my favorites questions to ask myself when I'm faced with a problem.

How can I keep this from happening again?

How can I do this faster next time?

What would happen if I _____ next time?

How can I be a better _____?

How can I learn this faster?

What decision would I have to make to _____?

How can I earn extra money to pay for _____?

How can I grow myself today?

How can I attract better people into my life?

Say for instance you just got out of a bad relationship. Asking yourself "how can I keep this from happening again?" is only the first part of problem solving. The second part of problem solving is brainstorming and writing down as many answers as you can think of and then implement one or all of them.

Problem solving unlocks endless possibilities! Stop telling yourself you're not artistic, could never work for that company, or couldn't start your own business, and start problem solving and practicing the skills necessary!

NEW BELIEF

I'm a motherfucking problem solver!

1

————⟨◆–◆–◆⟩————

A person's will is like water, it will go

around or through whatever it needs

to in order to get to where it wants to

go!

Barbie the Welder

————⟨◆–◆–◆⟩————

PLAY THE LONG GAME

I never was a patient person until I started my business. After a couple years as a full time artist I stopped asking how long is this going to take and started asking myself how far can I take this? I started playing the long game.

The long game is all about creating a solid foundation and security, and that takes patience and time.

Impatient people make mistakes and mistakes can be costly. Take a deep breath and slow the fuck down. Rome wasn't built in a day and neither will your empire! When you slow down you get to enjoy the journey.

Through all the doubt, hardship and fear keep moving forward. Some days you will move very little but keep moving forward. When you are running down a dream some days you may need to crawl but no matter what KEEP MOVING FORWARD! Its learning to have a long game mentality that helped me be happier, knowing if I work hard enough on the right things long enough I will accomplish everything that I want to and so much more!

NEW BELIEF

Slow is smooth and smooth is fast!

BLAST OFF!

— ◆ ◆ ◆ —

In the beginning there was Fuck You

Fuel, now there's just freedom!

Barbie The Welder

— ◆ ◆ ◆ —

Welcome to freedom my friend, true happiness! When you make the decision to live life on your terms, not be swayed by anyone's lack of belief in who you are, only look to yourself for your self-esteem, you truly live free and happy! Magic happens when you're living happy!

Just when you think life can't get any better, it does!

Even when something negative happens in your life, you will learn not to let yourself get down about it, in fact the more you practice the less things bother you!

You're a different person today than the person who first picked up this book! You are using your power for good, thinking differently, have better self-esteem, and are growing in the right direction! You deserve an incredible life, and I couldn't be prouder of you for putting in the work to make that happen! You never know whose life you can change by living in your truth!

Your rocket will always need fuel to continue its epic journey ever upward so make sure you are finding and connecting with likeminded people who are fueling their dream like you are! There are groups and pages on social media filled with positive uplifting people who want to see you thrive!

People either break down or they break through. You, my friend, have broken through to the other side!

FUCK YOU FUEL

NEW BELIEF

I'm Zen as fuck!

ABOUT THE AUTHOR

---◆-◆-◆---

Barbie The Welder is an American metal sculptor, published author, educator, and advocate for the skilled trades from Erin, NY. Even though she had no business experience or professional art education, Barbie's unique, self-taught style, quickly threw her into the spotlight on social media where she caught the eye of individuals and major corporations alike. To date she has designed and created sculptures for The American Welding Society, Harley Davidson, Miller Welders, Chicago Pneumatic, Carolina Shoe Company, and exclusive clients in 15 countries.

Barbie The Welder has inspired and taught thousands of people to weld art through her three books, Horseshoe Crafts, How To Weld Silverware Animals, and How To Weld Scrap Metal Art, and through her YouTube channel. In 2019 Barbie designed and created her first product line,

Metal Art Welding Kits, fun and easy welding projects that are perfect for learning to make metal art at home or introducing someone new to welding.

Barbie has welded sculptures live for audiences at shows and events including Americade Motorcycle Rally, Ridgway Chainsaw Carvers Rendezvous, Sturgis Motorcycle Rally, and SEMA Show in Las Vegas.

Barbie has also written The Inspiration Blueprint; How To Design & Create Your Inspired Life, and Honor Thy Art; How To Be An Extremely Successful Artist.

Visit BarbieTheWelder.com to view her gallery or request a commission, and connect with Barbie The Welder on Instagram, TikTok, Facebook, LinkedIn, and YouTube to see what she does next!